SKILLS FO

My Red
Face

Freda Gregory

supported by

north west arts board

First published & distributed by Gatehouse Books Ltd in 1995
Reprinted 2000 by Gatehouse Books Ltd
Hulme Adult Education Centre, Stretford Road, Manchester M15 5FQ
Printed by RAP, 201 Spotland Road, Rochdale
ISBN 0 906253 40 3
British Library cataloguing in publication data:
A catalogue record for this book is available from the British Library

Our thanks for their ongoing support to Manchester Lifelong Learning

Gatehouse gratefully acknowledges financial support from Manchester City
Council, North West Arts Board and Coopers and Lybrand.

The Beginner Reader Group: Chris Curley and Naznin Monaf have been
involved in all stages of this book.
Thanks to the following groups from Manchester Lifelong Learning for piloting the
early draft: Cambrian Centre, Chorlton Park Centre, Greenheys Centre.

Gatehouse is a member of The Federation of Worker Writers & Community
Publishers.

Gatehouse provides an opportunity for writers to express their thoughts and
feelings on aspects of their lives.
The views expressed are not necessarily those of Gatehouse.

Introduction

I was born in Manchester.
I had a basic education
while attending school.
I never really got to grips
with English.
In later life,
I decided to do something about this.
I attended evening classes for English,
achieving two MOCF* certificates.
I have completed Stages 1 and 2 of Wordpower**.
Hopefully, I will start studying
for my GCSE English this year.
I hope my book will encourage other students
to write their own stories,
and wish them well with their studies.
It is never too late to learn.

Thank you to tutors, Chris Riley and Sharon Jackson,
and to Gatehouse,
for this opportunity,
and to my husband for his support.

Freda Gregory

Manchester Open College Federation

City and Guilds certificate

In 1960 I started work
as a trainee sewing machinist,
making baby clothes.
I was just 15 years old,
very shy
and blushed
if anyone at work spoke to me.

I travelled by bus
to and from work
and found this very tiring
for the first few weeks.
After a month or so
I started to get used
to the travelling.

Work was great.

I made a friend,

and started to come out

of my shell

by talking to the older ladies

I worked with.

They were very helpful

and friendly.

Although I liked my work
I was always glad
when 5 o'clock came.
Work was finished
and I was ready to go home.

One particular night,
I was standing at the bus-stop
wondering what my Mam had cooked
for tea.
It might be chops
or my favourite
meat and potato pie.

The bus came,
and by this time
there was quite a queue.
I did, however, manage
to get a seat.
The bus filled up quickly
leaving standing room only.

A couple of people
were already standing,
when I heard someone cough.
I turned round,
it was my Dad.

I looked at him

and thought, "Oh, no,

he's three sheets to the wind."

In other words, drunk.

I stood up

and offered him my seat.

He said, "Hello Pop",

that was my nickname.

"You sit down,

I'll stand up."

"Stand-up," I thought,

"He couldn't stand sideways."

I sat there

and cringed with embarrassment

as he swayed to and fro.

As people were passing him

to get off the bus,

he made it difficult

for them

with his swaying

backwards and forwards.

People were pushing
into each other
and there was a lot of tut-tuts.
I sat there,
red in the face,
wondering
what the passengers were thinking
of my Dad.
Come to that,
what they were thinking
about me,
as it was obvious
we were related.

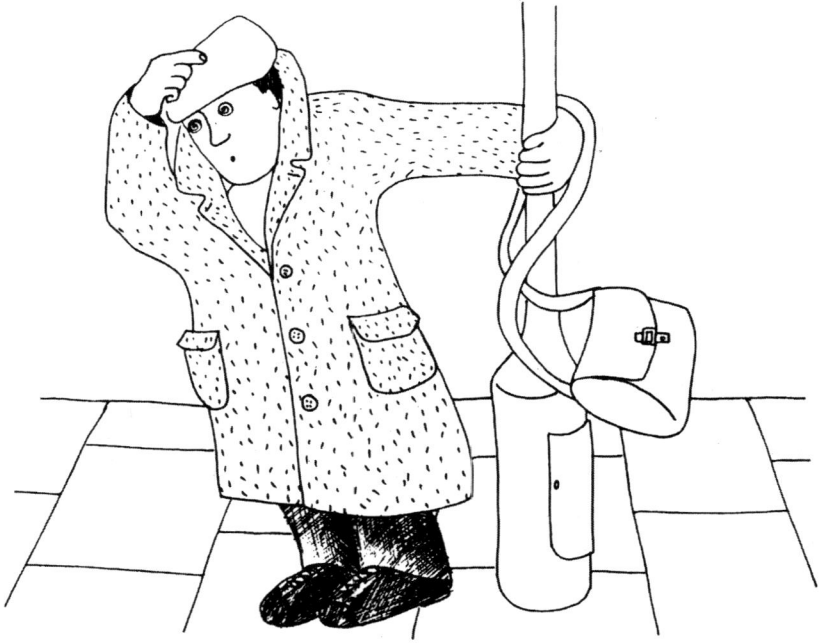

He was unaware
of what was going on
around him.
I couldn't wait
to get off the bus.
We got off the bus together,
but I left my Dad
and ran all the way home.

That bus journey
I will never forget,
although now
I can laugh about it.

Sadly,
my father died
19 years ago.
Yes,
he did have his faults,
as we all do.
Saying that,
I did love him,
and still miss him,
especially,
when I no longer hear him say,
"Hello, Pop."

Gatehouse Books

Gatehouse is a unique publisher

Our writers are adults who are developing their basic reading and writing skills. Their ideas and experiences make fascinating material for any reader, but are particularly relevant for adults working on their reading and writing skills. The writing strikes a chord - a shared experience of struggling against many odds.

The format of our books is clear and uncluttered. The language is familiar and the text is often line-broken, so that each line ends at a natural pause.

Gatehouse books are both popular and respected within Adult Basic Education throughout the English speaking world. They are also a valuable resource within secondary schools, Special Needs Education, Social Services and within the Prison Education Service and Probation Services.

Booklist Available

Gatehouse Books
Hulme Adult Education Centre
Stretford Road
Manchester M15 5FQ
Tel/Fax: 0161 226 7152
E-mail: office@gatehousebooks.org.uk
Website: www.gatehousebooks.org.uk

The Gatehouse Publishing Charity is a registered charity reg. no. 1011042
Gatehouse Books Ltd., is a company limited by guarantee, reg. no. 2619614